High Functioning

Luz Nunez

BookLeaf Publishing

India | USA | UK

Presentation by *BookLeaf Publishing*

Web: www.bookleafpub.com

E-mail: info@bookleafpub.com

ISBN: 9789358314267

First edition 2024

*My Son, you are the guiding light of my life.
I Love You more than words could ever
express.*

Free To Be

We all yearn to be
Free
To be Loved
To be Lost
To be Found
Free
To be Bold
To be Proud
To be Loud
Free
To be Joyful
To be Angry
To be at Peace
And all these things are within our reach.
To be Free
Is to be Me
Freedom is simply, to Be.

Your Daughter

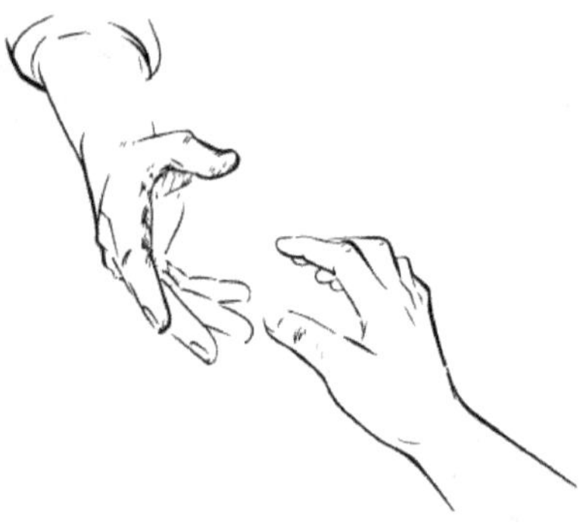

You prepared me for this.
To care for you when you are ill, old and weak.
To accompany you, in those times when friends are gone.
To be there for you, simply, because you are my Mom.

I've been left on my own
Since I can remember.
When you were here, time would never last.
All that is left now is time,
And lost opportunities that have now passed.

And then I wonder,
Who will care for me in my old age?
To accompany me when friends are gone?
To be there for me, like a Mother should.

If not you, then who would?

You prepared me for this.
I am your daughter
Left alone in the world, then and now.
You prepared me for this,
I am your daughter,
Who can live life on her own, somehow.

Does Anyone See

Does anyone see
that little girl
who cries herself to sleep
while others are tucked in,
and given a kiss on the cheek?

That little girl
who is brave enough to speak,
even after being punished for saying what she
thinks.

That little girl
who plays with plants and trees,
because they are there to keep her company.

Does anyone see
that little girl
who shows up everyday,
does her best at school and blows the others
away?

That little girl
with potential to shine bright
she is friendly, kind and quiet,
and always seems alright.

That little girl
who wonders what it's like
to have a loving family,
who hugs and holds you tight.

Does anyone see
that little girl
staring back at me
who wonders to herself,
Does anyone see me?

Hidden

Looking beyond today
is hard to see

Looking back in time
looks different to me.

Was I wrong,
was I right,
was I hidden in plain sight?

Looking back in time
the past reveals to me,
I was hidden behind an addiction that took over
me.

Looking beyond today
now I can see
a world without my vices,
and a chance to live free.

Drips

I speak for…
The drips in the faucet,
Who work their way to being of service for our
daily needs.
Cleansed and processed, funneled through pipes
and filters,
Taken for granted as the drips find their way
back to the sea.

Rivers

8

I speak for…
The rivers and streams flowing with ease
Through the streets, allies and levies made
As they are filled with rubbish, and broken
dreams,
We push you beyond your natural reach
For our convenience, and for our vanity.

Lakes

I speak for…
The lakes in the valleys,
Still with a majestic presence
While we drain you of your essence slowly over time.
And with it take away the livelihood of all that is left behind.
And we wonder why you cannot give any more,
After we took all you had and left a dry desert floor.

Oceans

I speak for…
The waters in the Ocean both feared and loved,
Larger than life whose power is powerless to the
destruction of mankind.
You bring us pleasure, provide us sustenance
and calm in the waves,
And in return we fill you with rubbish, pollute
you with chemicals and destroy the life you've
made.

Water

I speak for our Water…
That gives life to this earth
Who has been pushed, pulled, poisoned, taken
for granted by our fellow man
And will never return once we have taken all
that we can.

A Contradiction

I'm a contradiction,
both powerful and weak.
I'm a teenage Mom
who is stuck at seventeen.
Searching for my own support
while others count on me,
I'm highly educated
and still do stupid things.

Praised for my accomplishments
I hide my truth down deep.
My vices not only hurt myself,
it hurts those who believe in me.

I'm a contradiction,
both powerful and weak.
Humbled by addiction
that will not take over me.

Shame Part 1

I will not live in shame
Fearing the looks and whispers of who they
think I am,
Struggling with my own self-worth,
hiding the parts of me
that others look down upon because of what they
think. .

Pretending all is ok, and that there's nothing here
to see,
I keep it all together with each puff of smoke I
use to comfort me.

Why Can't I

Why can't I move past the trauma
Beyond the past, let it go?
Why does it linger,
Why does it come back,
Why does it still have a hold?

I know it has been there all this time,
Have tried to ignore it, it does not die.
Like an old memory still inside me
Or a shadow that will always haunt me.

Why can't I move past the trauma,
Why can't I move beyond time?
Like trying to escape a life that was never mine.

Why can't I move past the trauma
That everyone sees in me?
They stare, or smile, or stay clear,
It's heavy, this trauma, and a burden to bear.
I never asked for it to be here.
There are moments when it seems it's all in the
past,
Until it comes back, a relapse like the last.

Why can't I move past the trauma?

Will it ever go away?
What do I need to do to get this out of me,
How can I set myself free?

Why can't I move past the trauma?
It is here to stay?
Will there ever be a free day?
When I can celebrate all parts of me
Including the trauma that has made me.

Why can't I move past the trauma?

It is now clear to see,
this trauma is, and has always been, a beautiful
part of me.

High Functioning

Doing the most,
Seemingly easy,
Poised and polished,
By being deceiving.
Can others tell?
I'm going to hell?
The biggest lies,
I hide so well.

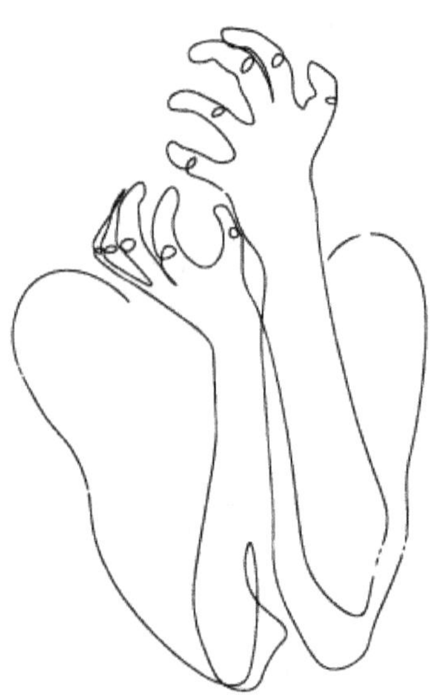

A Child Shook

Protect the child
Who grew up inside
Trying to find a place to hide.
If people would only stop and look
They would see a little child shook.
Needing love and comfort,
Appreciation and trust
But her only friends are in a book.

I can't let them see
That shaken child, the real me.
So I continue yearning for hope
Rolled up and gone,
in a puff of smoke.

Protect the Child

Protect the child
So that everyone can see
that she is smart, true, and worthy.
Deserving of love,
Like an open book
A simple acknowledgment
Is all it took.

Let Go

Tomorrow a new day comes
A new chance,
A new beginning,

And yet time still holds tight
Like it wants me to stay
Hidden in plain sight.

Looking beyond today
It's easy to see,
I must let go of time
So it can let go of me.

Shame, Part 2

I will not live in shame, I will accept my reality
That I'm imperfect, broken, and doing all I can,
Instead of hiding, I will love me for who I am.
All those parts of me deserve to be seen,
There is no shame in being me.

The End

21

The end is near,
Yet so far,
Tomorrow shows us who we are.
We pray we will see the day
To try again before we reach
The End.